ConTenTs

Welcome to our guide to the **BRILLIANT** game that is Among Us! With everything from hints and tips to fun games and puzzles, you'll find everything you could ever want to know about Among Us in these pages!

Victory

CONTINUE

Published 2022
Little Brother Books Ltd, Ground Floor, 23 Southernhay East, Exeter, Devon, EX1 1QL
Printed in the United Kingdom.
books@littlebrotherbooks.co.uk I www.littlebrotherbooks.co.uk

AMONG US EXPLAINED!

Everything you need to know!

What is Among Us?

Among Us is basically, a whodunnit mystery game set in space. At the start of the game, each player is given a role – most will be Crewmates, but at least one player will be an Imposter!

The Crewmates have a number of tasks to complete in various rooms around the map, while the Imposter is tasked with killing off the Crewmates before they can complete them all, and without being caught.

Every time a body is found, the Crewmates will have a meeting, at which they can choose to vote to eject the person they suspect is the Imposter. If they don't have any idea who the Imposter is, they can choose not to vote anyone off. If they vote to eject an innocent Crewmate, then the game continues.

Crewmates win the game by completing all their tasks OR identifying the Imposter (or Imposters) and ejecting them from the map. Imposters win the game by killing all the Crewmates OR preventing them from completing all their tasks.

It's a game of deduction – but luckily for you, we're here with some handy bits of advice on how to give yourself the best chance of winning – whether you're playing as a Crewmate or an Imposter!

Among Us 2022 Roadmap

A bit of history!

Among Us is the brainchild of Marcus Bromander, one of the founders of Innersloth. He used to enjoy a game called Mafia, a card game played in person. It was a murder mystery card game where one player would be assigned as a traitor. Everyone would spread out round the host's house, and the traitor would need to 'kill' each player by approaching them and running a finger across their throat without anyone seeing them.

Bromander took the idea and set it on a spaceship – the game's initial working title was actually SpaceMafia. The game was initially launched in June 2018 for mobile only, with a Windows version following at the end of the same year.

Without a big marketing budget, not many people learned about the game, but it quickly established a small but loyal following online. All that changed when the Covid-19 pandemic took root in early 2020. As people looked around for new games to play, a number of YouTubers stumbled across Among Us and helped reach a much bigger audience. Today, it has over 60 MILLION players active every single day!

The game is now also available on Switch, Xbox and PlayStation so however you like to play your games, you can join the craze!

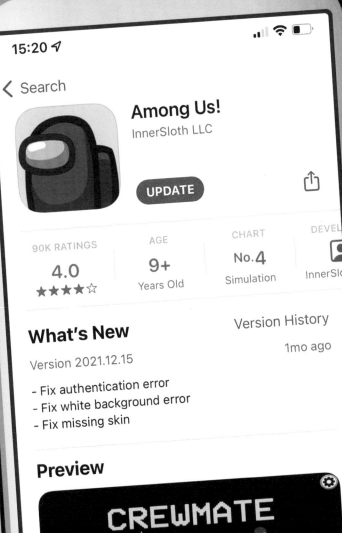

MULTIPLAYER MODES

All the different ways to play the game!

Local game

A local game is one where all the players can connect to the same network. One of you hosts, and everyone else connects without having to go online. This can be a fun way to play with friends at a party or sleepover, as you can hold your meetings in person! However, such opportunities are pretty rare, so most of the time, you'll be playing online. You might be able to do this over a school or college network during break times, however!

Private game

To join a private game, you will need to have been sent a code from the host. Only those with the code can join the game, so it's a great way to play a game that only features people you already know. Once you have been sent the code by a friend, you simply select Private Game and enter the code to be taken to the lobby where your friends will all be waiting for you.

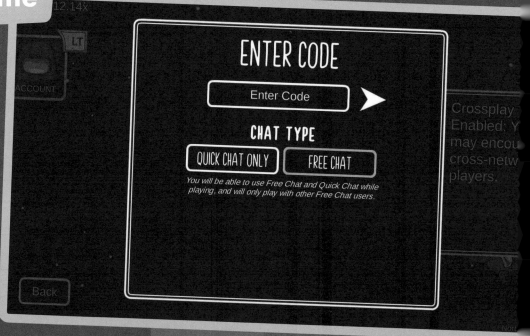

Public game

To join a public game, you simply need to scroll down the list to find a game with rules you like the sound of that has space for more players and hit join. To the right, you'll see how many spaces each game has.

Among Us makes it easy for you to find suitable games by allowing you to filter by things such as how many Imposters a game has, the language the game chat will be in, and which map you will be playing on.

One thing that is important to know is that you'll need to choose a game pretty quickly once you access the Public Game menu. Otherwise, the games on offer will fill up, and you'll be told the game is full. If this happens, refresh the menu to see the latest available games – and be quicker to make your choice this time!

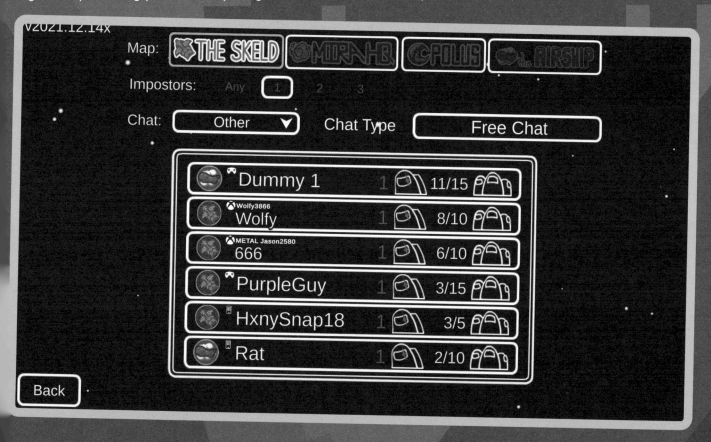

Hosting a game

If you're hosting the game, you get to choose all the rules and regulations for the game – you'll find more information about all the settings you can control on pages 6 and 7. You also get to choose whether or not you set it up as a private game – in which case you'll be given a code you can send to the friends you would like to join you – or a public game – in which case you will be joined by other Among Us players who find your game in the lobby.

GAME MODE
SETTINGS EXPLAINED

What are the best settings to use?

Imposters

For a balanced game, you will need a good balance of Crewmates to Imposters. Too many Imposters and the game becomes unmanageable, too few and it can become a bit dull. We recommend that you have one Imposter for up to eight Crewmates, and two Imposters if you have more than that. The maximum number of Imposters you can select is three, but things get chaotic if you choose three Imposters on any setting less than the maximum number of players!

Confirm Ejects

This will decide whether players will be told the player they voted off was an Imposter or not. Obviously, if you only have one Imposter in your game this is irrelevant, but it can make the game much more challenging if you have more than one Imposter and don't tell players if they guessed correctly. It is a setting that works best with experienced players only – anyone new to the game will get confused easily!

#Emergency Meetings

This is how many emergency meetings (extra meetings, basically) each player can call. It is set at one per player by default, which works perfectly. Choosing two tends to slow the game down too much, so we advise leaving it alone.

Your role is
Impostor

Player Speed

As this affects all the players in the game, there's not much difference to be made by changing this, so it is another one best left alone really.

Emergency Cooldown

This is how many seconds must pass before you can call another meeting. 20 seconds is a sensible limit but make sure it is LESS than the kill cooldown otherwise you might figure out who the killer is but be unable to vote them off before they strike again....

Discussion Time

This is how long players have to chat in a meeting before voting starts. It's up to personal preference, but allow at least 40 seconds to avoid players just making a wild guess. Longer times will allow for more discussion and more educated guesses, but too long makes things drag on a bit. Remember that discussion is added to voting time too.

Voting Time

30 seconds is usually enough for this task – any longer and you only slow things down for no good reason. As a rule, try to keep the time for discussion and voting to under two minutes combined.

Crewmate Vision

It tends to make games more fun if the Crewmates can't see quite as far as Imposters. Very low scores of less than 1.0 for this attribute can make the game really terrifying as you never know when you will bump into an Imposter!

Imposter Vision

Make this 0.5 or so longer than whatever attribute you choose for Crewmates for a well-balanced contest!

Kill Distance

This is how close an Imposter has to be before they can kill a Crewmate. The greater the distance, the more chance a Crewmate has to run away. For a nerve-wracking game, set a long kill distance and Imposter Vision, and short Crewmate vision so you can be bumped off without even seeing who did it!

Task Bar Updates

You can choose to turn these off altogether, see them only during meetings, or have them always on. We recommend having them set to always on.

Visual Tasks

This decides whether you get visual confirmation when Crewmates are performing certain tasks. Because Imposters can't perform tasks, this makes it easier to confirm a player is definitely a Crewmate. As such, is something to turn on for newer players, but turn off for more experienced players to increase the challenge.

Common/Long/ Short Tasks

This is the breakdown of how many of each task type you have. Common Tasks are useful as you can spot players not taking part in them, but avoid too many long tasks for a more dynamic game.

CUSTOMISING YOUR CHARACTER

Choosing the right look is an essential part of any videogame, and Among Us is no different!

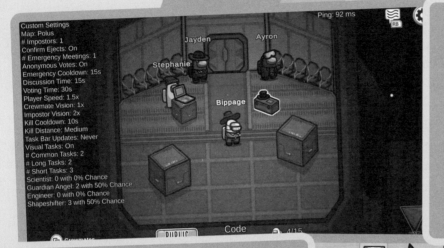

On the fly

As well as changing your avatar between games, you can make changes to your look in the lobby. Simply head to the computer on the desk while you wait for the game to start and you can make the same changes – but be quick as the game might start at any second, and you might not have completed the look!

Colour

You can choose the colour of your avatar, which is the key way other players will identify you. You can't be the same colour as another player, so if you are using the pregame choice, some options may not be available. If you enter a game where someone has already selected your preferred colour, then you will automatically change to another colour.

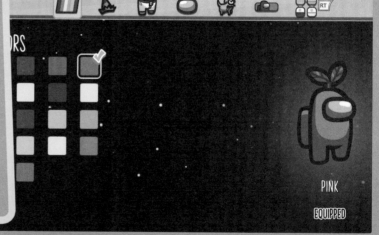

Hats

Hats can be a cool way to stand out, and more than one player can have the same hat on in a game – which means you're guaranteed to keep whatever you choose.

Skins

Like hats, more than one player in a game can wear the same outfit so combining this with a good hat choice is a sure-fire way to create a distinctive look for your avatar!

Visors

You can make cute additions to your visor with things like glasses to make your avatar really stand out!

Cosmicubes

These are a fun newer addition to Among Us! You can buy a Cosmicube using beans, the in-game currency. Each Cosmicube features a variety of cosmetics that you can unlock by earning more beans and spending them in the Cosmicube, with each choice you make unlocking further options. Some Cosmicubes are only available for a short time, but once you buy them, you will still be able to unlock its contents after it disappears from the store.

Pets

Pets can also only be purchased from the shop, and will also cost you money. Although they are pretty cool, it's important to remember there's no gaming advantage to having one so you don't need to invest. In fact, sometimes they can give you away when you play as an Imposter – a Crewmate might spot your pet trailing behind you as you flee your latest kill!

THE SKELD

The Skeld map is the original map, and is based on a spaceship travelling through outer space.

Vent Groups

- Admin / Cafeteria / Shields / Hallway
- Electrical / MedBay / Security
- Navigation / Weapons
- Weapons / Shields
- Lower Engine / Reactor
- Reactor / Upper Engine

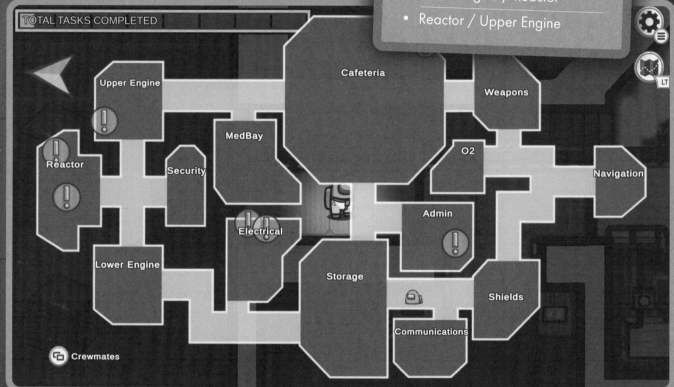

TOTAL TASKS COMPLETED

Upper Engine

Cafeteria

Weapons

Reactor

MedBay

O2

Security

Navigation

Electrical

Admin

Lower Engine

Storage

Shields

Communications

Crewmates

Victory

CONTINUE

Task Key

- **S** Short
- **L** Long
- **C** Common
- **V** Visual

Task List

ADMIN
- (S) Upload Data
- (C) Fix Wiring
- (C) Swipe Card

CAFETERIA
- (S) Fix Wiring
- (L) Empty Garbage
- (C) Download Data

COMMUNICATIONS
- (S) Download Data
- (S) Accept Diverted Power

ELECTRICAL
- (S) Calibrate Distributor
- (S) Divert Power
- (S) Clean Vent
- (S) Download Data
- (C) Fix Wiring

LOWER ENGINE
- (S) Accept Diverted Power
- (L) Fuel Engines
- (L) Align Engine Output

MEDBAY
- (V) Submit Scan
- (L) Inspect Sample

NAVIGATION
- (S) Chart Course
- (S) Stabilise Steering
- (S) Download Data
- (S) Accept Diverted Power
- (C) Fix Wiring

O2
- (S) Clean O2 Filter
- (S) Accept Diverted Power
- (L) Empty Chute

REACTOR
- (S) Unlock Manifolds
- (L) Start Reactor

SECURITY
- (S) Accept Diverted Power
- (C) Fix Wiring

SHIELDS
- (S) Accept Diverted Power
- (V) Prime Shields

STORAGE
- (L) Fuel Engines
- (V) Empty Garbage
- (V) Empty Chute
- (C) Fix Wiring

UPPER ENGINE
- (S) Accept Diverted Power
- (L) Fuel Engines
- (L) Align Engine Output

WEAPONS
- (S) Download Data
- (S) Accept Diverted Power
- (V) Clear Asteroids

Rasha left the game

Your role is
Impostor

Kill and sabotage

Crewmates

THE SKELD
PLAYING TIPS

Players will always start in the cafeteria in Skeld, which is one of fourteen rooms in total.

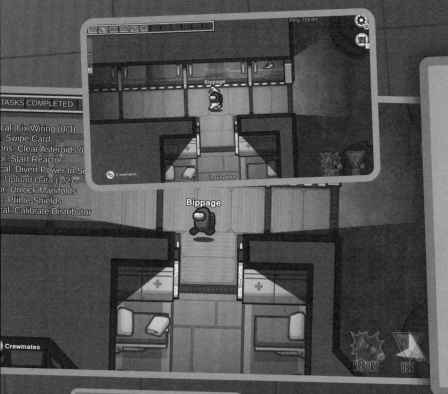

Keep on moving

The map is more or less a loop, with the corridors connecting the rooms in a circular way – only the Admin room which sits between the Cafeteria and Storage offers a slight variation on that route. As such, it is best to keep moving in a continuous circle when playing as a Crewmate. It makes no real difference whether you go clockwise or anti-clockwise, but if you keep the same general direction between meetings, you'll be able to complete your tasks in a logical order without having to go back on yourself all the time.

Visual Tasks

There are five visual tasks that will prove to other players you are not an Imposter. These are in Weapons (Clear Asteroids), Medbay (Submit Scan), Storage (Empty Garbage and Empty Chute) and Shields (Prime Shields). If you see other players in those rooms, it can be a great opportunity for you to prove your innocence to them. They can also be good places to see if other players leave those tasks – a possible sign that they might be the Imposter!

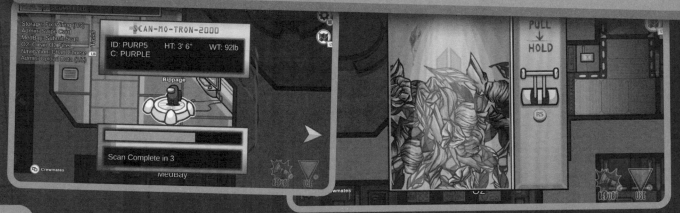

Vents

There are 14 vents on Skeld, which can come in very useful if playing as an Imposter. As always you need to make sure that you aren't spotted when using them, but there are two particularly useful areas where the vents operate in a triangle. These are between the Cafeteria, the corridor and Admin, and Security, Medbay and Electrical. By using more than one vent you can hop into a vent, kill a Crewmate, then hop into the other vent to end up in a different room altogether. It gives you much more mobility across three rooms if you use them wisely.

Electrical

Well connected

The circular nature of Skeld, coupled with the comprehensive vent system, means that most rooms have multiple exits available. That can be useful when playing as an Imposter as there isn't really an area where you can get caught having made a kill.

MIRA HQ

This level – set high on a Skyscraper – is small, but perfectly formed!

Vent Groups

- Launchpad / Reactor / Locker Room / Medbay / Balcony / Admin / Office / Greenhouse / Hallway / Laboratory / Decontamination

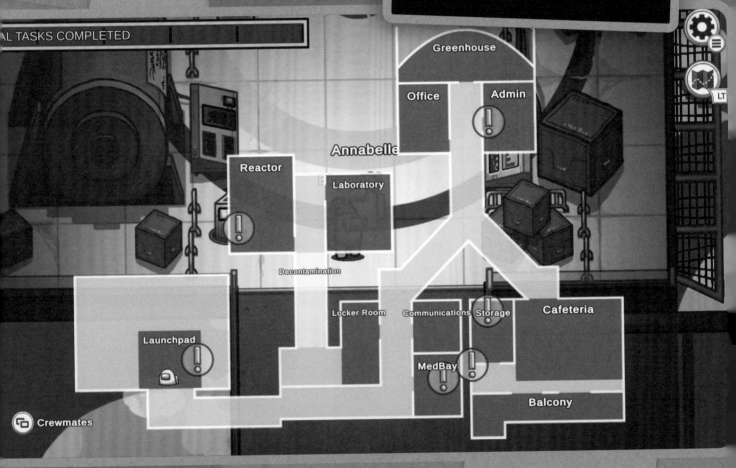

AL TASKS COMPLETED

Greenhouse

Office

Admin

Annabelle

Reactor

Laboratory

Decontamination

Locker Room

Communications

Storage

Cafeteria

Launchpad

MedBay

Balcony

Crewmates

Your role is
Engineer

Can use the vents

Task Key

- **S** Short
- **L** Long
- **C** Common
- **V** Visual

Crewmates

Task List

ADMIN

- **S** Prime Shields
- **S** Chart Course
- **C** Accept Diverted Power
- **L** Enter ID Code

BALCONY

- **L** Clear Asteroids
- **S** Measure Weather

CAFETERIA

- **S** Buy Beverage
- **S** Empty Garbage
- **L** Accept Diverted Power

COMMUNICATIONS

- **L** Accept Diverted Power

DECONTAMINATION

No Task

GREENHOUSE

- **S** Clean O2 Filter
- **L** Water Plants

- **L** Accept Diverted Power
- **C** Fix Wiring

HALLWAY

- **C** Fix Wiring

LABORATORY

- **S** Sort Samples
- **S** Assemble Artifact
- **S** Accept Diverted Power
- **C** Fix Wiring

LAUNCHPAD

- **S** Fuel Engines
- **S** Run Diagnostics
- **L** Accept Diverted Power

LOCKERROOM

- **C** Fix Wiring

MEDBAY

- **V** Submit Scan
- **L** Inspect Sample

OFFICE

- **S** Process Data
- **L** Accept Diverted Power

REACTOR

- **S** Unlock Manifolds
- **S** Divert Power
- **L** Start Reactor

STORAGE

- **C** Fix Wiring
- **L** Water Plants

GAME COMPLETE

Lvl 9

8

1 758

Locker Room

A Move through Vent
LS Vent Direction
Crewmates

Vents

Mira HQ has by far the most comprehensive system of vents of all the Among Us maps. You can get pretty much anywhere by venting quickly, covering vast distances and then escaping quickly. The smaller nature of the map does leave you slightly more likely to be caught however, with a greater risk of a Crewmate spotting you.

When playing as a Crewmate, be wary of those vents. They can leave you vulnerable to attack from an Imposter so play smart and stick together!

No security cameras

Mira HQ is the only map that has no security cameras at all. That means it is more important than ever to stay in sight of other Crewmates. Wandering off on your own in search of tasks to complete is a quick way to make yourself a target for a savvy Imposter. Throw in all those lovely vents and it's a recipe for disaster!

Launchpad

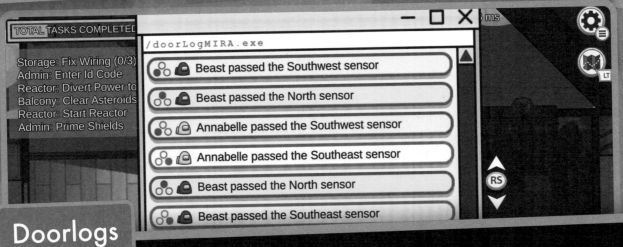

/doorLogMIRA.exe

Beast passed the Southwest sensor
Beast passed the North sensor
Annabelle passed the Southwest sensor
Annabelle passed the Southeast sensor
Beast passed the North sensor
Beast passed the Southeast sensor

Doorlogs

Mira HQ may not have security cameras, but it is still possible to keep a track of people remotely. Heading to the Communications room, you'll find a door log that tracks who has entered each room. Because the evidence stays in the log, you can see who has been moving where by tracking which rooms they have gone into.

If you see that player A enters a room, followed shortly by player B, then player A is discovered dead – well, it's time to point the finger of suspicion at player B!

However, be aware you can only trigger a door log once every five seconds, so a smart Imposter will enter a room then leave immediately to make a kill elsewhere, having left evidence that appears to show they are innocent!

TOTAL TASKS COMPLETED

Storage: Fix Wiring (0/3)
Admin: Enter Id Code
Reactor: Divert Power to Admin (0/2)
Balcony: Clear Asteroids (0/20)
Reactor: Start Reactor
Admin: Prime Shields

Tasks

LB

Ping: 145 ms

LT

Bippage

Aaaaaaaaaa

Claudiu

MedBay

Visual Tasks

Visual Tasks are normally a great way to prove your innocence to fellow Crewmates, as well as a good chance to isolate a potential Imposter. However, Mira HQ mixes things up a bit here, leaving only one – Submit Scan, in MedBay. Other tasks that are normally visual on other maps, such as Clear Asteroids, don't have visual components – so make sure you make the most of that MedBay when you get the chance!

Use the decontamination chamber

The Decontamination Chamber on the way to the Reactor is a gamechanger on Mira HQ, and one that favours Imposters. The doors will trap Crewmates in the corridor for a few seconds when they pass through, but Imposters can vent directly into the room. This makes it a perfect killing ground, and a great way to split up groups of Crewmates when you are playing as an Imposter!

Small but perfectly formed

Mira HQ is a small map, with only 14 rooms – and those rooms themselves are also pretty small. This can make it a hard map for Imposters as you're quite likely to bump into Crewmates as they move around the ship and it's easier to be caught in the act.

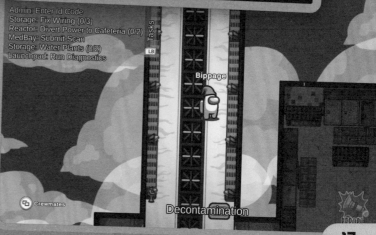

143 ms

Admin: Enter Id Code
Storage: Fix Wiring (0/3)
Reactor: Divert Power to Cafeteria (0/2)
MedBay: Submit Scan
Storage: Water Plants (0/2)
Launchpad: Run Diagnostics

Tasks

LB

Bippage

Crewmates

Decontamination

POLUS

Polus has both inside and outside areas to explore, with 15 rooms and lots of space.

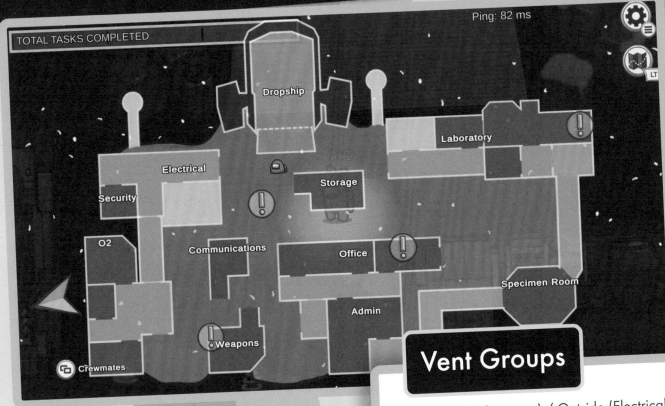

Ping: 82 ms

TOTAL TASKS COMPLETED

Dropship

Laboratory

Electrical

Storage

Security

O2

Communications

Office

Specimen Room

Admin

Weapons

Crewmates

Vent Groups

- Outside (Laboratory) / Outside (Electrical)
- Electrical / Outside / O2
- Laboratory / Admin / Outside
- Outside / Office Hallway / Storage

Your role is
Crewmate

Do your tasks

Task Key

 S Short

 L Long

C Common

V Visual

Task List

ADMIN

No tasks

COMMUNICATIONS

L Reboot Wifi

L Upload Data

DECONTAMINATION

C Fix Wiring

DROPSHIP

S Chart Course

C Insert Keys

ELECTRICAL

C Fix Wiring

L Download Data

LABORATORY

S Fix Weather Node

S Record Temperature

S Repair Drill

S Align Telescope

C Fix Wiring (right)

C Fix Wiring (left)

MEDBAY

V Submit Scan

L Inspect Sample

O2

S Empty Garbage

S Monitor Tree

S Fill Canisters

L Download Data

C Fix Wiring

OFFICE

L Download Data

L Replace Water Jug

C Scan Boarding Pass

C Swipe Card

C Fix Wiring

OUTSIDE

S Record Temperature

L Fix Weather Node

L Fuel Engines

L Open Waterways

SECURITY

No Tasks

SPECIMEN ROOM

S Store Artifacts

S Unlock Manifolds

L Download Data

L Start Reactor

STORAGE

L Fuel Engines

WEAPONS

V Clear Asteroids

L Download Data

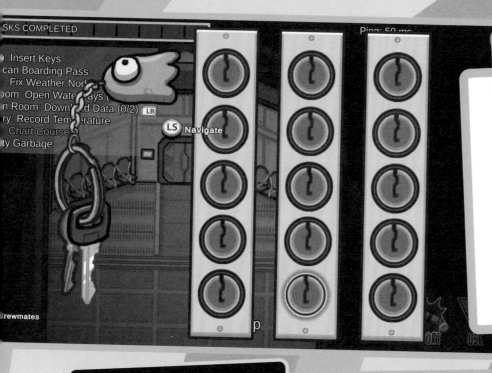

Insert keys

Immediately behind all Crewmates as they spawn in Dropship, the 'Insert Keys' task can be a real giveaway. If it's on the task list, most players will go straight to do the task – anyone who doesn't do it will look suspicious and may be an Imposter. If you ARE an Imposter, then make sure you at least look busy!

Use the cameras

The security cameras on Polus are the most comprehensive in the game, with six different screens to flick between. You can use these cameras when playing as an Imposter to identify targets too – look for people on their own and then vent your way to them quickly to get the kill.

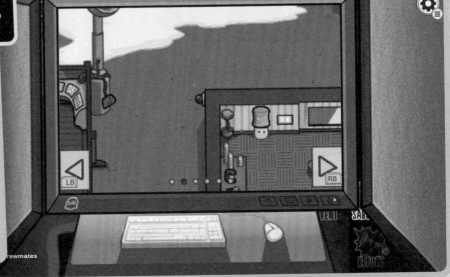

Stay close

Polus is a big map, and tends to lend itself better to the Imposters as it is easy to isolate players from each other. When playing as a Crewmate, try to stick in groups for safety's sake. It's worth suggesting it in meetings too, so that all the Crewmates work together. If you have fewer than 8 players on Polus it becomes very difficult so try to stick to games with more players available.

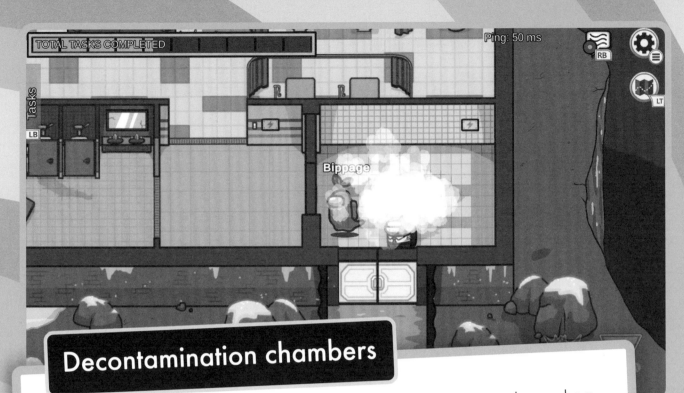

Decontamination chambers

The decontamination chambers on Polus only allow one player in at a time and so can be a good chance to kill players as they exit, because they'll be on their own by definition. However, if you are playing as an Imposter, it looks sus if you spend too much time hanging around them so be careful not to make it too obvious.

Vent groups

Get to know the four vent groups, especially when playing as an Imposter. They aren't very well connected so you can't zip around the map like you can on some levels. When you are playing as a Crewmate, stick to the south and southeast of the map as there are fewer vents there so you're safer from a surprise attack!

Were you born in a barn?

Polus features doors that can be closed by sabotage, slamming them shut and leaving players trapped in a room. Cunning Imposters can make the most of this by trapping a player in a room with them, killing them, then venting out. Be quick to leave though, because you'll be the prime suspect if someone else fixes the doors and you're discovered alone in a room with a body!

AIRSHIP

The Airship is the biggest of all the maps in Among Us with 18 rooms and 12 vents as well as ladders and a moving platform!

Vent Groups

- Vault / Cockpit / Viewing Deck
- Engine Room / Kitchen / Main Hall
- Main Hall / Gap Room / Gap Room
- Showers / Records / Cargo Bay

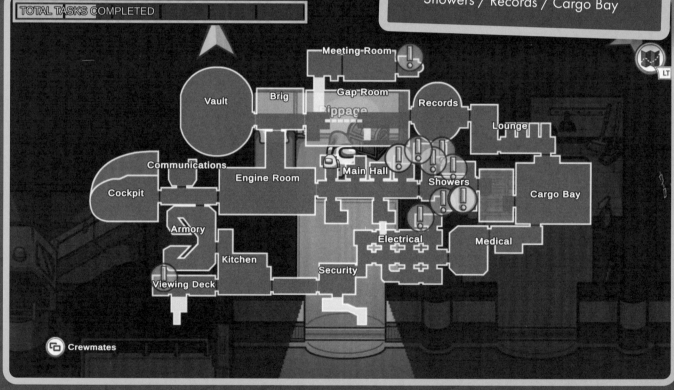

Task Key

S Short

L Long

C Common

Task List

ARMORY

- S Put Away Rifles
- S Put Away Pistols
- S Accept Diverted Power
- S Download Data

BRIG

- S Upload Data

CARGO BAY

- S Download Data
- L Fuel Engines
- L Unlock Safe
- C Fix Wiring

COCKPIT

- S Accept Diverted Power
- S Stabilise Steering
- L Upload Data

COMMUNICATIONS

- S Download Data

ELECTRICAL

- S Calibrate Distributor
- S Divert Power
- L Reset Breakers

ENGINE ROOM

- S Accept Diverted Power
- L Fuel Engines
- C Fix Wiring

GAP ROOM

- S Download Data
- S Accept Diverted Power

OUTSIDE

- L Upload Data

RECORDS

- S Download Data
- S Sort Records

SECURITY

- L Rewind Tape

SHOWERS

- S Accept Diverted Power
- S Fix Shower
- S Pick Up Towels
- L Empty Garbage
- C Fix Wiring

VAULT

- S Download Data
- S Polish Ruby
- S Dress Mannequin

VENTILATION

- L Start Fans

VIEWING DECK

- S Upload Data
- C Fix Wiring

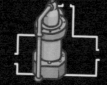

Kitchen   **Engine Room**   **Records**

Time remaining: 9

Confirm
Cancel
Navigate
Crewmates

Starting point

You can choose between three starting locations (which are random each time) so it's worth getting to know the map! If you're playing as an Imposter, you might luck out and start in a room with only one Crewmate – in which case act quickly to get a risk-free kill!

Security cameras

The good thing about the security cameras on Airship is that one of them is focused on the user. This means you can see if anyone is sneaking up on you, something that isn't possible on the other maps.

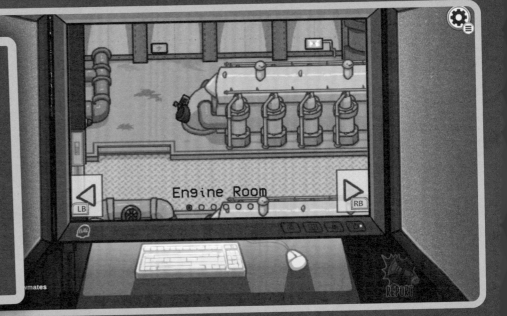

Engine Room

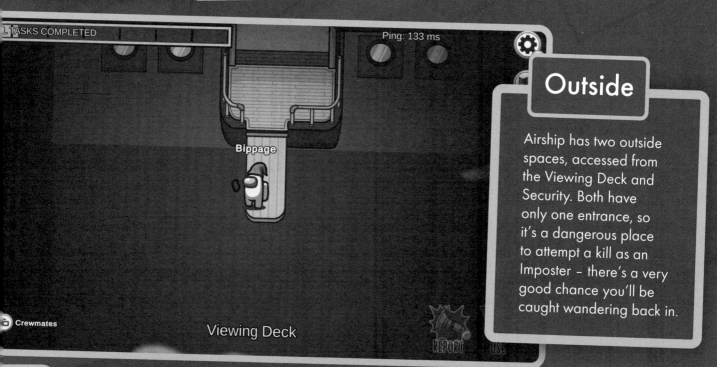

TASKS COMPLETED

Ping: 133 ms

Bippage

Viewing Deck

Crewmates

Outside

Airship has two outside spaces, accessed from the Viewing Deck and Security. Both have only one entrance, so it's a dangerous place to attempt a kill as an Imposter – there's a very good chance you'll be caught wandering back in.

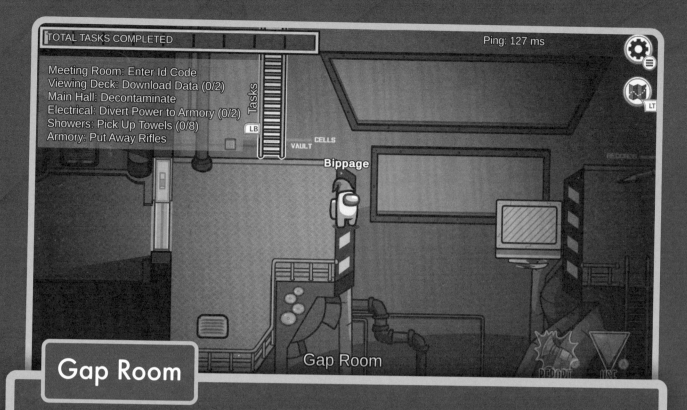

Gap Room

The moving platform in the Gap Room is your enemy in this game. It doesn't automatically return once it has been used, so it's easy to enter the room and be trapped – leaving you with no alternative but to retrace your steps and navigate around the problem.

That causes two problems – firstly, if you're rushing to fix a sabotage, you'll find yourself at a dead end and having to retrace your steps. Secondly, if you're followed by an Imposter, you can be left with no escape!

That means the Gap Room is often one that is best left alone completely!

Electrical

This is another danger spot for Crewmates, and a valued hiding place for Imposters. The nooks and crannies in the room make it impossible to see the whole room at once, offering plenty of hiding spaces for Imposters to make the most of!

Visual

There are no visual tasks on Airship – the only map where that is the case. As such, you will need to watch your colleagues closer than ever to see who the Imposters might be – because they won't be able to prove it with their actions!

BEING AN IMPOSTER!

Bumping off Crewmates without being caught is a risky business! Here are some top tips to give you an advantage.

No witnesses

When you're lining up a kill, make sure that there is no-one else in the room – just you and your intended victim. If there are people around to witness the crime, they'll accuse you – and if they are persuasive with their argument, you might find yourself ejected. Try to carry out your kills in a room with more than one exit, whether that is doors or vents and look out for security cameras – if they are blinking red, then someone is watching!

Don't frame others too early

If someone sees you making a kill and identifies you, blame them to make it sound like a double bluff. Other than that, avoid making too many accusations early on in the game. Not only does it look suspicious, if you convince everyone another player is the Imposter and they are ejected, the others will realise you aren't to be trusted. Keep false accusations to the latter stages of the game where it can make a real difference and help you win the game without time to get caught out.

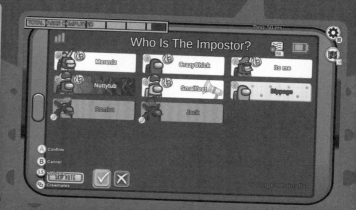

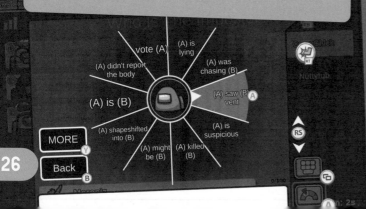

Don't vote too quickly

If you constantly vote before there's even been a conversation, you will draw attention to yourself. Let others lead the conversation, and if someone else accuses another player, support that player with your vote. Other than that, don't be afraid to skip voting, especially in the early stages.

Vent with care

Vents are useful, but an easy way to get caught if you're spotted entering or leaving them. Use them sparingly, and ideally only to carry out or escape from a kill.

Self-report sometimes

Self-reporting when you are the Imposter is a risk, because it immediately places you at the scene. However, it can be a good way to divert attention from yourself – just don't do it too often and be prepared to be accused of the crime yourself!

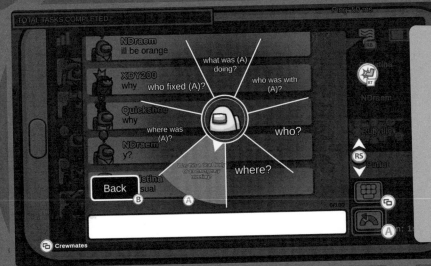

Play dumb

Act like a noob as much as you can. Even if you have a high ranking, claim you don't play this map very often, and act confused about which room is which. Ask simple questions and people will quickly start to ignore you – not knowing that you are in fact the evil genius behind it all!

Look helpful

Do what you can to look like everyone else! Pretending to carry out tasks and spending time looking at security cameras are good ways to blend in – but don't overdo it or you stand more chance of being found out!

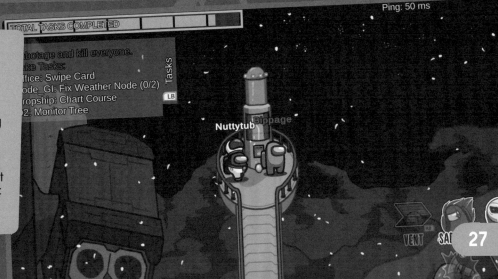

Spotting an
IMPOSTER

This is what life as a Crewmate is all about – spotting the Imposters and then ejecting them from the ship! Here are some important things to remember!

Write things down!

There's a lot going on in Among Us, and in some of the bigger games, it can become a real headache keeping track of who did what. So go old school! Keep a notepad handy and jot things down as you notice them. It will stop you forgetting important clues as to who the Imposter might be!

Keep track of who is where

Keep a note of who you see in which room, and what they were doing. For example, if you see two players in a room or headed towards a room, then one of them is reported dead – you can make an educated guess about the other player. You can use the map to see where people are, and this can be a handy guide too.

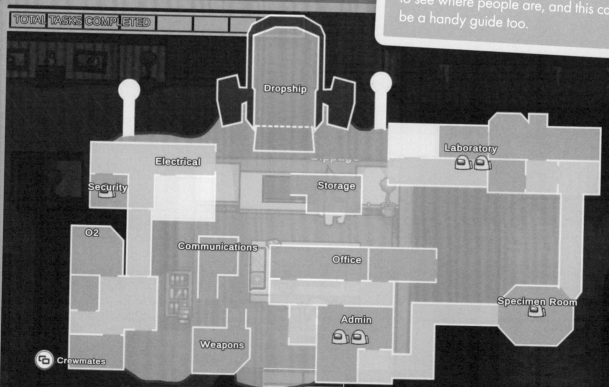

Look out for people near bodies

Very often, the person nearest a body is the Imposter. If you enter a room and there is a player standing near a body and they haven't reported it yet, the odds are that you have caught the imposter red-handed. This is also the case if you pass someone leaving a room as you enter it, and you then find a body.

Sometimes people do make honest mistakes and not see a body, but remember – Crewmates need to check rooms for lurking Imposters. Doing so properly means they are unlikely to miss something as obvious as a body, so it could be a sign that they aren't who they appear...

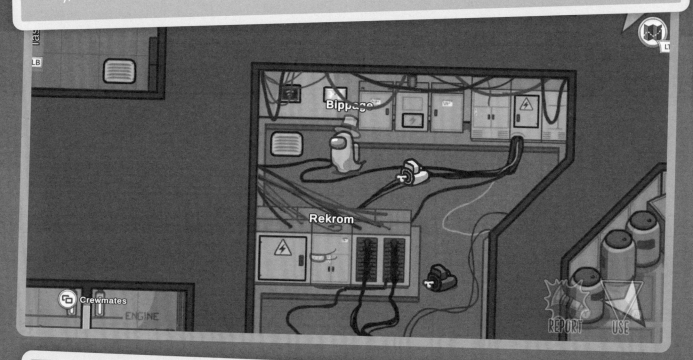

Learn the tasks

If you know which tasks are where, you'll find it easier to catch out an Imposter in questioning. If someone says they were emptying the garbage in a room where there is no such task, for example, you can catch them out. To do so effectively, you'll need a good knowledge of the tasks themselves (though our maps have a handy key to help you out!)

You can also catch out Imposters if they stand near tasks and PRETEND to do them – if you know a task should take a long time and they appear to have finished it too quickly, then it's another big clue!

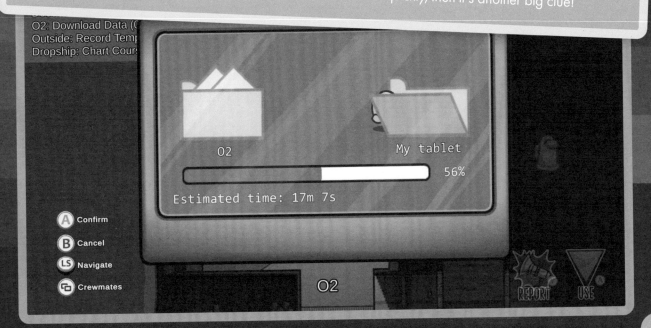

Look out for loners

If there's one thing Imposters can't stand, it's company. Too many people around make it virtually impossible for them to complete their dastardly mission, so look out for players who seem a little too keen to get away from a big group.

The opposite is also true – Crewmates will naturally be worried about being on their own too much in case the Imposter gets them. If you see a player who seems a little TOO happy to wander round on their own, it could be that they have nothing to fear so subconsciously, they play the game in a different way.

Don't get too close

Following suspects in Among Us has one major drawback – if the person you are following to see if they are the Imposter IS the Imposter, you're making it very easy for them to make you their next target. To that end, keep a safe distance back from anyone you strongly suspect to be an Imposter, keeping them in sight but not close enough to bump you off.

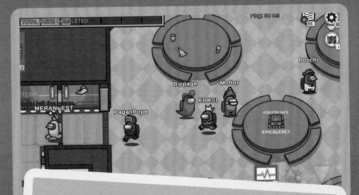

Stay in sight

While it's a good idea not to get too close to a suspected Imposter, be aware that they will try and lure you somewhere quiet before turning on you and killing you. To avoid that, stay in sight of other players too – if they can see you, and you can see the Imposter carrying out a kill, they can back you if the Imposter tries to frame you. There's nothing more frustrating than catching an Imposter in the act and then they convince everyone that YOU'RE the one that should be ejected!

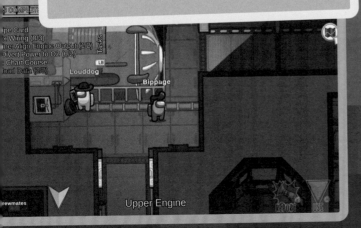

Look out for vent use

Always check to see if Engineers are part of the game – if not, then anyone using a vent is definitely an Imposter. This is very obvious if you see them entering or leaving a vent with your own eyes, but there are other ways to figure out if someone is practising such dark arts. If you check a vented room with one door and find it empty, for example, the only way a player can then exit that room is if they used a vent. Similarly, if players seem to be moving around too quickly – they go from being in a room behind you to emerging from one in front of you, for example – then they may well have used a vent to achieve it.

Watch the taskbar

Sometimes, an Imposter will pretend to be a Crewmate by mimicking completing a task. However, watch them carefully. If the taskbar is visible in the game (most games have it set to on as a setting) then you'll see it increase as the task is completed. If the player you are watching gets their timing wrong and walks away from the task without the taskbar rising, then you might have found your Imposter!

Monitor meetings closely!

Look out for players who are too quick to accuse others of being the Imposter, especially before there has been a discussion, or if they don't appear to have a solid reason for their suspicions.

In particular, Imposters can often slip up by claiming they saw a player killing another – but then that player is ejected and is shown NOT to be the Imposter. If that's the case, then their lie has been exposed and you should bring it up at the next meeting – along with any other evidence you manage to gather!

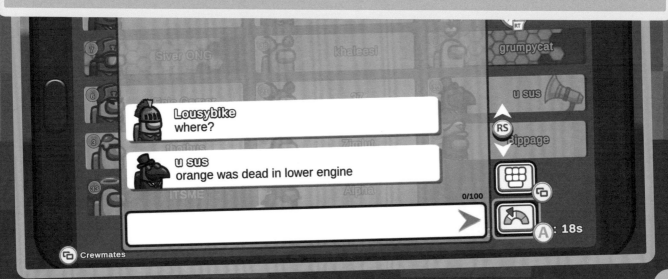

HOW TO BE THE PERFECT CREWMATE

Spotting the Imposter isn't the only part of being a good Crewmate. You'll need to complete tasks and work as a group if you are to succeed.

Fix sabotages

Sabotages can win the game for the Imposter if they aren't repaired quickly, so make sure you play your part in repairing them. As soon as one is identified, get moving to fix it. Try to avoid being isolated on the way to doing so, in case the Imposter is lying in wait to get you on the way. Staying in sight of other players is a good idea – and remember, if you don't help repair sabotage attempts, you'll look sus to the other players too!

Don't be afraid to skip votes

Voting for someone just because they've been accused with no evidence isn't helpful. Making random guesses will be more likely to eject innocent players, and it is in Crewmates' interest to keep as many players as possible on board.

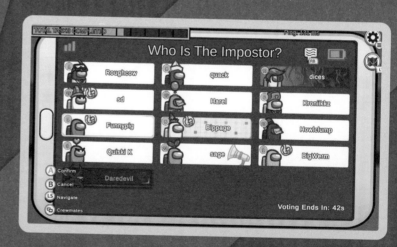

Make the most of visual tasks

Visual tasks are ones where your fellow Crewmates can see you completing them. We've compiled a list of them on each map page to help you find them easily. If you have a visual task, make sure you do it in front of another Crewmate. Imposters can't complete tasks so this will be proof to that Crewmate (or Crewmates) that you can be trusted and relied on. That will make them more likely to back you up if you get accused in an emergency meeting.

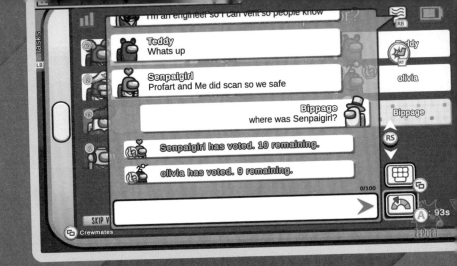

Speak up for others

The same is true if you are sure someone is NOT an Imposter. Maybe you've been following someone long enough to know they couldn't have been responsible, or you've seen them complete a visual task. If that's the case, tell everyone else. It's in your own best interests to keep genuine Crewmates on board the ship!

Focus on the tasks

If you dedicate all your time to identifying the Imposter and don't complete the tasks, the Imposter will win anyway! Make sure you allocate enough time to tasks so that the Imposter has to keep taking risks to win the game. If all the Crewmates ignore the tasks, there's less need for the Imposter to risk revealing themselves in the first place – and they'll still win!

Stay in groups

Sounds obvious, but if you're on your own, you're a sitting duck. There's safety in numbers, or at least in sticking close to well populated areas. If you're in an area that people pass through a lot, an Imposter would be taking a risk in bumping you off. A group is even safer but look out for anyone trying too hard to get you on your own – instead, try and stick with more than one player for safety. The exception is if you have seen a player completing a visual task and you know they are safe – though they might find it suspicious if you keep following them!

Follow suspicious players

If you think a player looks dubious, and don't like the answers they give in the meetings, then follow them round to see what they do and where they go. Keep a safe distance, however, unless there are other players around. If you find yourself in a situation where you and another player have seen each other performing visual tasks, you can become a powerful pair!

GUIDE TO EMERGENCY MEETINGS

Surviving without being killed by the Imposter is only half the challenge – you'll also need to be able to navigate your way through emergency meetings!

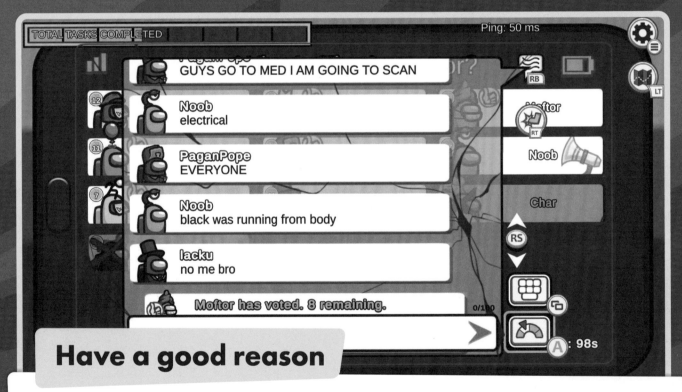

Have a good reason

Emergency meetings are called when someone finds a body (which is always a good reason) but they can also be called by hitting the emergency meeting button (the location of which varies from map to map). If you decide to call an extra emergency meeting, you'll need to have a good reason for doing so. The finger of suspicion is nearly always on the player that calls an extra meeting, so be prepared to be disbelieved.

For that reason, you'll need a good reason, such as seeing a player venting or witnessing a kill. Even then, be aware that the player you accuse will turn the tables on you and say that it is YOU who is the suspicious one, and you've called the meeting because THEY had found YOU out. If you do see someone venting, you don't need to call the meeting immediately. Sometimes it is best to gather more evidence and share suspicions first.

Don't call them too often or too early

Emergency meetings interrupt the flow of the game, so they are often limited to only one meeting per player (though it can be up to 9). If you have multiple uses of emergency meetings, don't overdo it. Other players are likely to vote you off just because you are annoying them, so be careful.

Similarly, calling an emergency meeting right at the start can cause problems too. You look incredibly suspicious, even if you feel like you have a good reason, and will often be voted out – so use them carefully!

Give as much detail as you can

"I saw Red kill Blue!" will get you nowhere. All that will happen is that Red will counterclaim that they saw YOU killing Blue and you put yourself in a tricky position. Instead, try to give as much detail as you can when making an accusation. Say where you were, what you were doing, and which players were near to you at the time. The extra detail will make you seem much more believable and make it more likely that others will listen to your opinion.

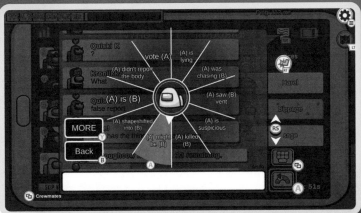

Pay attention to accusations

If other players are making accusations on flimsy evidence or voting for players before there has been much discussion, then it is highly likely they are an Imposter. Keep an eye on voting patterns and general conversations. For example, if Blue is very vocal that Red is the Imposter and persuades the group to vote for Red, only for it to transpire that Red is NOT the Imposter – well, that means Blue is quite possibly the person you need to vote off next.

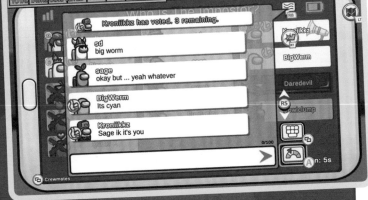

Don't be afraid to skip voting

It's no good sitting on the fence for the whole game, of course, but it is not in your interests to vote off Crewmates so only vote when you are pretty sure. The more Crewmates there are, the more chances there are for someone to see the Imposter in action or catch them out.

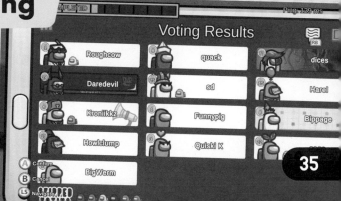

SMILE!
YOU'RE ON TV!

The CCTV cameras can be a great help in spotting Imposters. Here's how to get the most out of them!

Where are they?

You'll find CCTV in the security rooms of Skeld, Polus and Airship. There is no CCTV in Mira HQ. They'll grant you access to the security cameras on each map – there are four on Skeld, six on Polus and six on Airship.

Little and often

The first problem when using CCTV is that you will be defenceless while using them. You can only see the screen, so there's nothing to stop the Imposter strolling up behind you! As such, use them in short sharp spells so that you aren't taken by surprise, or by teaming up with another player that you know you can trust.

Switch cameras

Because the camera you are looking through will blink red, an observant Imposter will notice they are being watched. For that reason, it's usually more effective to switch between cameras frequently to catch the Imposter out. If you can only view one camera at a time, such as on Polus, switch frequently. If you can view them all, such as on Skeld, step away from the console then back to it again after a few seconds to lull Imposters into a false sense of security

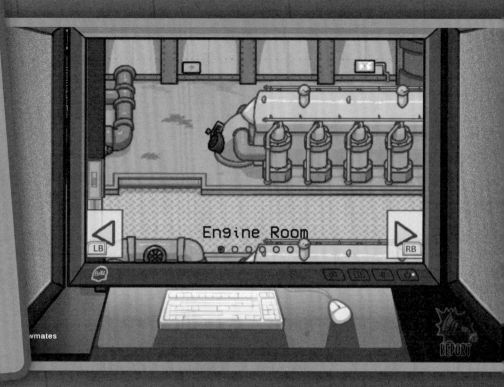

Don't spend all your time on the cameras

Sometimes, it can be useful to work as a team to make sure the cameras are being watched to keep players safe. This is especially true towards the end of the game where players might want to complete the last few tasks in a group while being watched on camera for extra safety.

However, for the most part, dip in and out of camera use. It's more effective to concentrate on completing tasks. Staying at the CCTV points will often annoy your fellow Crewmates as well as making it easy for an Imposter to figure out where you are and sneak up on you!

How to play in the
NEW ROLES

An exciting recent update to Among Us was the introduction of new roles. Here is how to make the most of them!

Shapeshifter

The Shapeshifter is the only new role for the Imposter – but what a role it is! If you are a Shapeshifter then you can copy the appearance of any other living crewmember for a short time. This enables some devious strategies to be employed, such as deliberately being caught in the act while appearing to be someone else and watching as they are then ejected.

However, if anyone sees the transformation you'll give yourself away so you need to choose when to use that skill very carefully indeed. You also need to be careful not to be seen in the same room as the person you are imitating, and to get somewhere quiet when the effect wears off so that you can change back without being noticed.

Engineer

At first glance this can seem like a really handy role as it allows the player to travel around the map quickly using the vents. However, being seen doing so can make others assume that YOU are an Imposter. You can use it to try and zip around the map to catch the Imposter by surprise but more often than not, it will end up with you being spotted and accused, so exercise these powers with care!

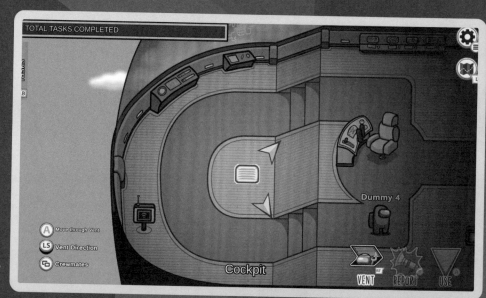

Scientist

If you are playing as a Scientist, then you're able to view all the other players' vital signs at any point, meaning that you'll know who is alive and who is dead at any point. If you see a player's signs drop, then you can immediately call an emergency meeting before the body is even found, which may help other players identify who was near the victim before the Imposter has a chance to slink away.

Try to remember who was with who as best you can, and check in on vital scans to see that they are still alive. For example, if you leave a room containing two players then seconds later your scanner shows one has died, then the other is probably the Imposter. If you had to wait for the body to be found, it would be much harder to prove it – but scanning vital signs is a big help.

The only problem is the batteries aren't great – so use with care!

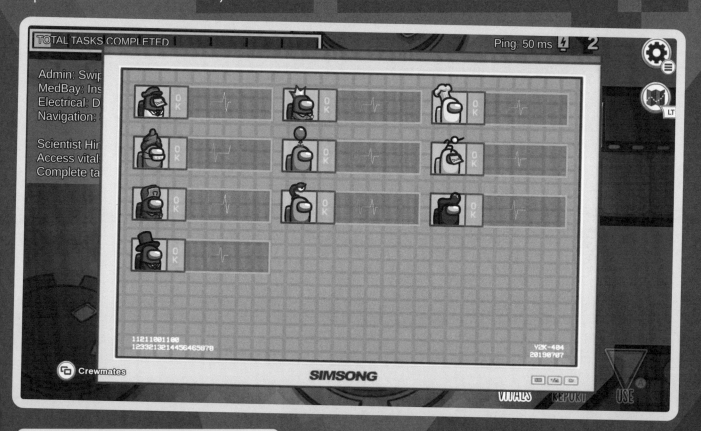

Guardian Angel

This ability means you can cast a protective shield over an opponent – but you can only do it after your own death! You can't vote in meetings or talk to other players, but of course, by being killed, you'll know the identity of at least one Imposter. If you're playing a game with only one Imposter, you can really ruin their day by following them round and casting shields on players they appear to be stalking – but be selective as they don't last long and there is a cooldown between uses!

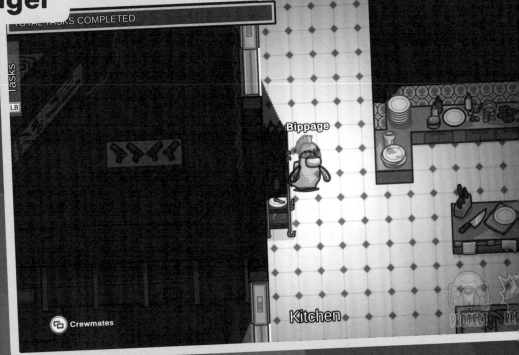

Among Us Puzzle Time!

Let's see how much attention you've been paying, Crewmates! Solve these two fiendish puzzles using information from this book, otherwise the Imposters will bump you off!

```
Y C A M E R A Q X K U J Q Z B
A S E C U R I T Y I D Y J S S
S U T E L Q O G M A J H M F F
D E C O N T A M I N A T I O N
B P P I A W T A R Q W P X M X
J O W I N G N F A J J A W A U
H L Z M E D B A Y V K K H I A
T U U G C R E W M A T E J V D
L S E N G I N E E R A J D P O
F S K E L D C X A T M T Y J G
X A K C A I R S H I P Q K V L
Q G S R X R Y A U E F G I F C
I S C I E N T I S T I Q H C K
N T E M I E L E C T R I C A L
B B I M P O S T E R K M A U N
```

Word search

Find the following words in the wordsearch, running left to right or top to bottom!

POLUS	ELECTRICAL	CREWMATE
AIRSHIP	MIRA	MEDBAY
IMPOSTER	SKELD	CAMERA
DECONTAMINATION	SCIENTIST	
SECURITY	ENGINEER	

Crossword

Solve the clues to complete our crossword and unlock the Decontamination doors!

Across

2 A game type where you need a code to join (7)

5 A bad guy in Among Us (8)

6 _____ Bromander, the creator of Among Us (6)

8 An Among Us Map with lots of outside space (5)

9 Among Us player that needs to complete tasks (8)

Down

1 The original Among Us map (5)

3 The studio that launched Among Us (10)

4 The real-life game Among Us was based on (5)

7 A room where you might find the CCTV station (8)

10 The company the Crewmates all work for (4)

FORTNITE

Among Us isn't the only game where you need to eject an Imposter!

VICTORY
THE IMPOSTORS HAVE BEEN EXPOSED!

DEFEATED IMPOSTORS

8 EMI130510   1 BANANAMAN9612

Voice chat

You can now play Fortnite with voice on through the game, with eliminated players only able to talk to each other while the others try and figure out who the imposter is.

Epic's answer to Among Us

Epic dropped its own version of Among Us, called Impostors, as a standalone game mode completely out of the blue in August 2021. It certainly caught Innersloth out, as the Among Us creators hadn't even been approached about collaborating on the project. Victoria Tran, Innersloth's community director went as far as tweeting how disappointed she was with Epic not asking to work together. She has a point – imagine how cool Among Us skins would be in Fortnite!

In any case, the game not only arrived – it arrived to stay. Unlike Limited Time Modes that disappear after a short while, Impostors was a permanent addition to the Fortnite roster, and it has been very popular. This is thanks in part to the fact that players still gain decent levels of XP in the game mode, which is unusual for anything outside the Battle Royale format in Fortnite.

IMPOSTORS

What's it all about

The premise is the same as Among Us, with eight Agents and two Imposters in each game. The Agents need to identify and expel the two Imposters while completing tasks on the only playable map – The Bridge. When a player is killed, they leave a fragment behind – those who find the fragment can call an emergency meeting, just like in Among Us.

Imposters can kill agents, but can't complete tasks, and it's up to the Agents to use the meetings to make accusations and provide evidence that gets the Imposter ejected. Unlike Among Us, you can also communicate in the game, using emotes to ask another player to follow you, for example, which makes staying safe easier.

In many ways, the Fortnite version is even better than Among Us, due to the improved dialogue – though the map is quite big and Imposters do seem to win more often than not. Give it a go and see what YOU think!

Choose your own adventure

Before each game, you can use the console in the lobby to indicate your preferred role. However, you can use this to your advantage. Watch what other players do – you can see the console over their shoulder. If someone is asking to be an Imposter, you'll know. It's not guaranteed that they WILL be an Imposter when the game starts, but it is still a pretty useful clue!

FACTS and FIGURES

Here are some of the coolest things you need to know!

It took a team of 3 people 12 months to create the game.

INNERSLOTH

15 June 2018 – the date Among Us was officially launched!

Among Us
Innersloth LLC
Contains ads · In-app
100M+
4G
4.4★
M reviews

Since it was launched in 2018, the game has been downloaded more than 530 MILLION times!

The busiest time ever for Among Us was in October 2020, when it had over 60 million people playing each day, with up to 3 million playing at the same time! Just imagine if there was only one Imposter!

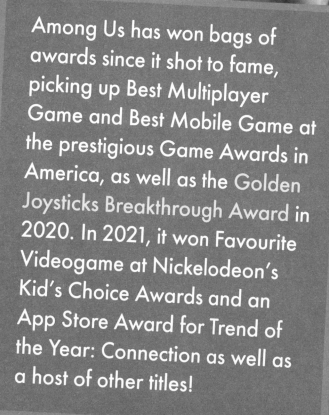

Among Us has won bags of awards since it shot to fame, picking up Best Multiplayer Game and Best Mobile Game at the prestigious Game Awards in America, as well as the Golden Joysticks Breakthrough Award in 2020. In 2021, it won Favourite Videogame at Nickelodeon's Kid's Choice Awards and an App Store Award for Trend of the Year: Connection as well as a host of other titles!

The first gamer to really popularise Among Us was Sodapoppin, an American streamer with over 3 million followers on Twitch. From there, Among Us's following just grew and grew!

Among Us is so popular that Innersloth cancelled plans for Among Us 2 in favour of making more changes to the original game instead!

Staying safe ONLINE

Like with any online game, it's important to stay safe when playing Among Us so you can concentrate on the important bit – having fun!

Play with friends

You can join public games, which will pitch you into a game against complete strangers, or play private matches, where players need a code to join. Private matches are by far the safest way to play – arrange with your friends a time to play online, and send the code to everyone. You can then play without any strangers involved. This can add more fun to the game because you will learn how your friends behave, helping you to deduce who is an Imposter and who is not.

If you are invited to a friend's private game with a code, don't share it with anyone else without asking the game host first.

Tell an adult

If you see or hear something that feels wrong, tell someone you trust. If someone online says or does something that makes you feel uncomfortable, you shouldn't keep it to yourself. However small it might seem, it's always best to be safe and tell someone.

Be careful about using other apps

It's quite popular to use apps like Discord while playing Among Us, allowing players to talk to each other in voice chat. You don't need to do this – you can communicate fine via the chat settings in the game. You should particularly avoid using voice chat apps with people you don't know.

Be careful about making purchases

You can pay to remove ads in mobile versions of the game, or to buy some accessories such as pets – but be careful when doing so. Always ask the permission of whoever's credit card is stored on the device you are playing on. If you have your own card, try to avoid using a debit card as you will have less protection if money is stolen from it – use a credit card instead. Nothing you can buy in Among Us makes you any better at the game, however – everything is purely cosmetic so go with it.

Join games that are using quick chat

Playing in games that use Quick Chat is the safest way to get involved with Among Us. This limits players to choosing from pre-selected communication options, so means there is less chance of anyone asking you for personal information or saying anything rude or hurtful. Free Chat does filter out most rude words, but it is easy to sneak them through by slightly misspelling them, so it is best avoided if you want the safest and most enjoyable online experience.

Play somewhere you can be seen and heard

It's tempting to hide away in your room and play in solitude sometimes, but it's best to play games somewhere in the house you can be seen and heard by an adult. That way, if someone does or says something inappropriate on screen, they will be there to help you immediately. It means there is less chance of you being exposed to anything that would upset you.

Teach a grown-up how to play

Take some time to get your parent or guardian involved in the game too! Teach them how the game works and what it is about so they understand what you are doing and can ask any questions they want to about the game.

40 Wordsearch

```
Y C A M E R A Q X K U J Q Z B
A S E C U R I T Y I D Y J S S
S U T E L Q O G M A J H M F F
D E C O N T A M I N A T I O N
B P P I A W T A R Q W P X M X
J O W I N G N F A J J A W A U
H L Z M E D B A Y V K K H I A
T U U G C R E W M A T E J V D
L S E N G I N E E R A J D P O
F S K E L D C X A T M T Y J G
X A K C A I R S H I P Q K V L
Q G S R X R Y A U E F G I F C
I S C I E N T I S T I Q H C K
N T E M I E L E C T R I C A L
B B I M P O S T E R K M A U N
```

41 Crossword

Across:
2. PRIVATE
5. IMPOSTER
6. MARCUS
8. POLUS
9. CREWMATE

Down:
1. SKELD
3. INNERS
4. MAFIA
7. SECURITY
8. POLOH
10. MIRA